Jezebel

and the Goddesses

Mitsi Burton

Jezebel & the Goddesses, by Mitsi Burton
Copyright ©, 2000

ISBN # 0-89228-084-0

Published by
Impact Christian Books, Inc.
332 Leffingwell Ave.,
Kirkwood, MO 63122
314-822-3309

Contents

Introduction

Jezebel is a name that evokes seduction, lust, intrigue... It describes a controlling, scheming, sensual woman. A woman who manipulates to her advantage. A woman of expensive taste. An egocentric woman who would, if she could, make the very atmosphere, and all of its contents, rotate around her. A woman who puts her desires, which are many, before the needs of others. A jealous, covetous woman, who feels the need to have something another person has. A woman of subtlety who could destroy a life with her insinuations and her power to influence minds. A willful woman who, to obtain what she wants, would resort even to witchcraft.

There is a spirit known as Jezebel which follows this pattern. It is a complex spirit, a principality. This spirit has a fondness for women. Women are the abode of its preference. There is hardly a woman to be found who is not sheltering a Jezebel spirit, to a greater or lesser degree. However, it is not beyond the spirit of Jezebel to take up residence in a masculine body. Behind transvestites and cross-dressers, there is a Jezebel spirit provoking such behavior. Among homosexuals, Jezebel plays havoc with jealousy, gossip and intrigue. It may be surprising, but this spirit is sometimes also found in straight men.

1

The Historic
Queen
Jezebel

Ahab was King of Israel between the years 874-853 before Christ. At that time, Ethbaal was the king of Tyre and Sidon. Ethbaal (notice the name of Baal within his name) had a daughter named Jezebel. Ahab married princess Jezebel in disobedience to God, because she was not from among the tribes of Israel. Instead of Ahab converting Jezebel to his religion, Jezebel converted Ahab to hers. Jezebel introduced the worship of Baal into Israel, and brought 450 prophets of Baal and 400 prophets of Ashera to the palace, where they "ate at the table." Ahab also ordered images of Ashera to be made and put them in places of worship.

8

*And in the thirty and eighth year of Asa king of Judah
began Ahab the son of Omri to reign over Israel:
and Ahab the son of Omri reigned over Israel in
Samaria twenty and two years. And Ahab the son of
Omri did that which was evil in the sight of Jehovah
above all that were before him. And it came to pass,
as if it had been a light thing for him to walk in the
sins of Jeroboam the son of Nebat, that he took to
wife Jezebel the daughter of Ethbaal king of the
Sidonians, and went and served Baal, and worshipped him. And Ahab made the Ashera; and Ahab
did yet more to provoke Jehovah, the God of Israel
to anger than all the kings of Israel that went before
him.*

1 Kings 16:29-33

Jezebel ordered that all the prophets of God be
killed. Obadiah, the head of the royal household, hid one
hundred of the prophets of God in a cave and fed them.
God told Elijah, who thought he was the only remaining
prophet of God, to meet with Ahab. At this meeting, Elijah
asked Ahab to send all his prophets, the prophets of Baal
(450) and the prophets of the groves, that is, the prophets of Ashera (400) to mount Carmel. A great miracle of
God happened there. When the people of Israel saw the
miracle, they realized who the real God was. Elijah then
told the people of Israel to bring all the prophets of Baal
and Ashera to him, and he killed them all. (1 Kings 18:
7-40) When Jezebel heard about this, she swore to have
Elijah killed. (1 Kings 19: 1,2)

The Personalities of Ahab and Jezebel

The Scripture reveals Ahab's and Jezebel's true character in the story of the vineyard of Naboth. Ahab wanted to have a vegetable garden, and he decided that the vineyard adjoining his palace was the right place for his garden. The problem was that the vineyard had an owner, and it was not for sale, so Ahab had a temper tantrum:

And it came to pass after these things, that Naboth the Jezreelite had a vineyard, which was in Jezreel, hard by the palace of Ahab king of Samaria. And Ahab spake unto Naboth, saying, Give me thy vineyard, that I may have it for a garden of herbs, because it is near unto my house: and I will give thee for it a better vineyard than it; or, if it seem good to thee, I will give thee the worth of it in money.
And Naboth said to Ahab, The Lord forbid it me, that I should give the inheritance of my fathers unto thee. And Ahab came into his house heavy and displeased because of the word that Naboth the Jezreelite had spoken to him: I will not give thee the inheritance of my fathers. And he laid him down upon his bed, and turned away his face, and would eat no bread.
1 Kings 21: 1-4

Jezebel came to see what was happening to Ahab, and he told her. Ahab could not deal with his problem. Just like a child who sees a toy in the hands of another child and wants it, even when his parents may offer him other toys, in this same way Ahab wanted the vineyard.

And Jezebel his wife said unto him, Does thou now govern the kingdom of Israel? arise, and eat bread, and let thine heart be merry, and I will give you the vineyard of Naboth the Jezreelite.

1 Kings 21: 7

Ahab permitted Jezebel to solve a problem he should have solved himself. He should have considered another piece of land or forgotten about a vegetable garden. He was rich, and did not need to grow his own produce. He just wanted entertainment, a toy.

Jezebel then took control of the situation in order to solve Ahab's problem. She wrote letters to the authorities of the city in Ahab's name and sealed them with Ahab's seal (Deception). She had contrived a plan to get the vineyard (Scheming, Manipulation). She bought two false witnesses that would give testimony against Naboth and so be able to have him stoned to death (Deception, Murder).

And it came to pass, when Ahab heard that Naboth was dead, that Ahab rose up to go down to the vineyard of Naboth the Jezreelite, to take possession of it.

1 Kings 21: 16

Ahab did not do a single thing, either good or bad, until the problem was solved for him. Then, and only then, he got up from his bed, and then only because he was getting his toy.

Ahab Is Cursed

Elijah the prophet received word from God telling him to go to the vineyard of Naboth, where Ahab had gone to possess it:

And thou shalt speak unto him, saying, Thus saith the Lord, Hast thou killed and also taken possession? And thou shalt speak unto him, saying, Thus saith the Lord, in the place where dogs licked the blood of Naboth shall dogs lick thy blood, even thine.

And Ahab said to Elijah: Hast thou found me, O my enemy? And he answered: I have found thee, because thou hast sold thyself to work evil in the sight of the Lord.

Behold, I will bring evil upon thee, and will take away thy posterity, and will cut off from Ahab him that pisseth against the wall and him that is shut up and left in Israel. And will make thine house like the house of Jeroboam the son of Nebat, and like the house of Baashan son of Ahijah, for the provocation wherewith thou hast provoked me to anger, and made Israel to sin. And of Jezebel also spake the Lord, saying, The dogs shall eat Jezebel by the wall of Jezreel. Him that dieth of Ahab in the city the dogs shall eat, and him that dieth in the field shall the fowls of the air eat.

1 Kings 21: 19-24

Notice that although Jezebel was the author of the plan, God considered Ahab responsible for the kill-ing of Naboth. Ahab let Jezebel do whatever she wanted, and was happy that she was solving his problem. He did not come up with the plan; he did not write the letters; he did not obtain and pay the false witnesses, yet God ascribed the guilt to him as well as to Jezebel.

> *But there was none like unto Ahab, which did sell himself to work wickedness in the sight of the Lord,* **whom Jezebel his wife stirred up.**
>
> *1 Kings 21: 25*

When Ahab heard of the curse, he rent his clothes, dressed in sackcloth and fasted. God saw it:

> *And the word of the Lord came to Elijah the Tishbite, saying, Seeth thou how Ahab humbleth himself before me? because he humbleth himself before me, I will not bring the evil in his days; but in his son's days will I bring the evil upon his house.*
>
> *1 Kings 21: 28, 29*

The Throne of Israel Is Taken from the House of Ahab

Ahab died and his sons inherited the throne. Joram, one of his sons, was king when Elisha received a word from God. Elisha told one of the young prophets to find Jehu, son of Jehoshaphat. When Jehu arrived, Elisha called him into a private room to anoint him king of Israel.

And he arose, and went into the house; and he poured the oil unto his head and said unto him, Thus saith the Lord God of Israel, I have anointed thee king over the people of the Lord, even over Israel. And thou shall smite the house of Ahab thy master, that I may avenge the blood of my servants the prophets, and the blood of all the servants of the Lord, at the hand of Jezebel. For the whole house of Ahab shall perish: and I will cut off from Ahab him that pisseth against the wall, and him that is shut up and left in Israel, and I will make the house of Ahab like the house of Jeroboam the son of Nebat, and like the house of Baasha the son of Ahijah: and the dogs shall eat Jezebel in the portion of Jezreel, and there shall be none to bury her.

2 Kings 9: 6-10

Joram the king was at Jezreel, when a guard on a watch tower saw Jehu and his troops coming. Joram sent a messenger, and then another, to inquire if Jehu was coming in peace. Joram and the king of Judah who happened to be visiting, went out in their chariots to meet Jehu and they reached him in the vineyard of Naboth:

And it came to pass, when Joram saw Jehu, that he said, Is it peace, Jehu? And he answered, What peace, so long as the whoredoms of thy mother Jezebel and her witchcrafts are so many?

2 Kings 9: 22

Joram turned to flee, and Jehu shot an arrow right

through his heart. Jehu told his aide to throw Joram's body into Naboth's vineyard, and leave it there. Jehu then continued moving toward Jezreel.

Death of Jezebel

And when Jehu was come to Jezreel, Jezebel heard of it; and she painted her face, and tired her head, and looked out at a window. And as Jehu entered in at the gate, she said, Had Zimri peace, who slew his master? And he lifted up his face to the window, and said, Who is on my side? who? And there looked out to him two or three eunuchs. And he said, Throw her down. So they threw her down: and some of her blood was sprinkled on the wall, and on the horses: and he trod her under foot.
And when he was come in, he did eat and drink, and said, Go, see now this cursed woman, and bury her: for she is a king's daughter. And they went to bury her: but they found no more of her than the skull, and the feet, and the palms of her hands.

2 Kings 9: 30-35

It seems that Jezebel thought that she could seduce Jehu with her beauty and she prepared for it. However, Jehu was not impressed.

Take notice of this Scripture. It will help you in casting out Jezebel. You can read it to the demon to weaken her.

2

Jezebel and Ahab Spirits

The Work of the Spirit of Jezebel

The first time I went to minister deliverance, I had an encounter with a spirit of Jezebel. The lady I was called to pray for was having **marriage problems**, and was thinking about **divorce**. Jezebel was responsible for this. It took both a morning session and an afternoon session, and when finally the Holy Spirit revealed to me that Jezebel was hiding in her female organs, the demon had to leave. By that time, I had already cast out pride, haughtiness, jealousy, control and other spirits that work under Jezebel, but the principality kept resisting until the Holy Spirit intervened.

I Had a Jezebel Spirit

I had already received deliverance at Hegewisch Baptist Church, and did not recall Jezebel being cast out of me. However, I did find out about Jezebel and what she does to the character of a woman, making her rebellious and **not submitted** to her husband. The way Jezebel does this is by speaking thoughts into her mind such as, "He is stupid", "He is not worth a dime", etc. So I made a conscious decision to behave and think exactly the opposite of the way Jezebel would have liked me to behave and think. Any impulse or thought that I suspected came from her, I would cast down and resist.

A few months later the Lord started giving me names of demons that I needed cast out from myself. The second one he gave me was Jezebel. I kept writing the names down, and when I did not hear anything else, I made an appointment with my pastor for deliverance. My pastor had never ministered deliverance, but I requested it and told him I would help him. I brought the list of names and told him to start calling out the first one and commanding it to go in the name of Jesus.

The pastor did as I told him and the first demon, Rebellion, manifested and then left. The pastor, because of his inexperience, did not realize that the first demon was already gone and continued to command it to go. The second demon, Jezebel, manifested and was very disturbed that the pastor was not calling her out by her right name. She sat up very straight and proper, and coldly told the pastor: *"I am not Rebellion!"* Surprised, the Pastor asked: *"And who are you?"* Proudly, she answered: "Jezebel." (For those who are not acquainted with deliverance, let me explain that when a demon manifests, sometimes it makes the person's body move in a way related to its manifestation. In this case it was in proud and arrogant body language. The demon also makes use of the person's speaking ability to talk to the minister.)

When the pastor commanded her out, she started bargaining with him, saying: *"Let me stay, I am not doing anything here any longer. She will not listen to me. She will not do what I tell her to do."* The demon had felt the impact of my attitude toward her. She did not want to leave and considered my attitude a bargaining point. Demons always resist leaving, and some will plead and reason with the minister to let them stay. The minister, of course, should ignore the requests of the demon and continue commanding it out. Jezebel had to leave. All the others demons in the list appeared in sequence and also left. Thus, I learned that when the Holy Spirit gives you a list of names of demons, the demons also know about it and they stand in line in the same order of the list, waiting to be cast out. Sometimes when I cast out a demon, even without a list of names, I command the "next demon in line" to manifest and it does.

Does Every Woman Have a Jezebel Spirit?

Since I minister primarily to women. I have cast out many Jezebel spirits. However, I still have not ministered to a woman who did not have a Jezebel. It may be a stronger or a weaker Jezebel, but it has always been found. Sometimes it has manifested on its own, other times I have to command it to manifest, and it does. When I minister to a woman that has come to me for other problems, in addition to casting out the demons related to the other problems, I always confront and cast out the Jezebel spirit.

When I am casting a Jezebel out (after casting out all the demons under her control) I ask the Lord to send the eunuchs to "throw Jezebel out of the window" and I also ask for the angels to bring the dogs "to eat Jezebel up." Also, I ask the Lord for the spirit that was in Jehu to come, riding his horse, to trample Jezebel. Jezebel gets frightened and becomes weaker when I use this tactic. While ministering recently, I asked the Father for the dogs and the manifested Jezebel told me very quickly: "I am not going to jump out the window!" I had not even mentioned the window!

Where did I get all this? The Holy Spirit told me to do it. It is based on the Scriptures. Refer in this book to the Historic Jezebel chapter, under "Death of Jezebel"

The Counterpart of Jezebel

The Biblical counterpart of Jezebel in a man is Ahab. When there is a strong spirit of Jezebel in a woman, look for the spirit of Ahab in the husband. An Ahab type of man might find the Jezebel type of woman attractive and gravitate toward her. He looks for the strength of the Jezebel spirit to shield his own weakness.

Recently I ministered to a woman with marriage problems. The husband was present while I ministered to her. When Jezebel manifested she pointed to the husband and said that she would not leave, because "he gave her strength."

When a woman with a strong Jezebel spirit marries a man with an Ahab spirit both spirits may get stronger. If the spirit of Jezebel in the wife is very strong, the spirit of Ahab in the man would have to be very strong also if there is going to be a balance in the marriage. Trouble starts in a marriage when the woman has a strong Jezebel, while the husband resists an Ahab. The woman tries to control the husband and his decision-making, while the husband fights for his rightful place in the marriage. The demons interact with each other to provoke their hosts to strife and marriage-breaking.

Ahab imparts weakness and lack of responsibility to a man. When the Ahab spirit is the strong one in a marriage, the man leans on the woman and wants her to make all the decisions that he should be making and sometimes even wants the wife to be the bread-winner. This situation is very stressful for a woman with a weak Jezebel spirit, since she will not enjoy having to take control of the decision-making. She will be forced to face situations, sometimes embarrassing, that the husband does not want to face even when he is the one who caused the situation. She will be pressured to solve the problems that he does not want to solve, and this will make her very unhappy. The woman will feel insecure and unprotected. She will resent being married to an Ahab type man, because she expects him to be the head of the household and make all the tough decisions, and will feel unhappy if he does not. This also leads to strife and marriage-breaking.

Even if the woman is a professional, or a career

woman, when she gets home she expects the husband to deal with things like getting a plumber, getting the car fixed and the gutters clean. The woman prefers to solve laundry, cooking and shopping problems. I speak from experience, I am a graduate architect and worked in the architectural field many years. But when I got home, I wanted my husband to handle those kinds of problems while I preferred to deal with the traditional feminine type of things.

If a strong non-Ahab husband rules over a Jezebel wife, she may exercise her controlling spirit over the children or other relatives.

3

Jezebel's Witchcraft

Because of her willfulness, a Jezebellic woman will turn to witchcraft to get things going her way. If she cannot obtain her desires by natural manipulation and control, she will resort to the supernatural to obtain her goals.

If the Jezebellic woman becomes a Christian, and is not delivered of the spirit of Jezebel, she could easily become a Charismatic Witch. She will turn to prayer to get things done her way, thinking that it is the Christian way to get what she wants and to override the will of others.

When Christians do not believe that a Christian can harbor demons, they of course, do not seek deliverance. They will be tormented with diverse impulses and desires that they know are not right, and because they cannot believe that they are fighting a demon within themselves, they will continue suffering. Some Christians let the spirits of pride, arrogance and "Holier than Thou," make them proud and arrogant. Some are tormented by spirits of lust and pornography, and many times lose the battle.

Other Christians fight Ahab and Jezebel. They hear sermons about the husband being the spiritual head of the household, about the submission of the wife to the husband, and they applaud and say, "Amen," but when they get home it is back to the old routine of the husband letting the wife run the show.

The Christian woman is affected by Jezebel just the same as a non-Christian woman. If she belongs to a denomination that does not believe that a Christian can have demons, she will be battling urges to control and dominate, urges to be the center of attention, and urges to be proud and arrogant. She will be wondering why she is the way she is, and feels the way she feels. And when it comes to the need she feels to get her way, she will probably not even resist that urge. She will be willful about getting her way, and that willfulness will be carried over into her prayer life. She will pray that things be done her way. She will not stop to consider the will of God. And this is dangerous.

Charismatic Witchcraft

Several years ago, I used to attend a weekly prayer meeting. The lady who leads it belongs to a Pentecostal denomination that does not believe that a Christian can have demons. The lady has a very strong character, is quite domineering, and after a year or so of attending, I began to feel uncomfortable and quit going to the prayer meeting.

When I found out about deliverance, I went to Hegewisch Baptist Church for a deliverance workshop. I received deliverance and was amazed at the demons that came out of me. I felt that the circle of Christians that I had been worshipping with needed to know about it. What I wanted them to know was that Christians, obviously, could have demons in them. I thought that it was urgent for them to become informed. However, I was in for a strange experience. Instead of being excited about finding this out, they were horrified and wanted nothing to do with it.

One of the people I called was the leader of the prayer meeting. She heard my story on the phone, making little noises: "Humph!" "Humph!" during the conversation. When I finished, she said: "If you had demons cast out of you, you are not Christian."

I asked her "But, didn't you see me at your meeting every week, praising God?"

She said: "Yes, you looked like a Christian, but you are not Christian."

I did not argue with her. But I continued receiving deliverance, and also continued ministering it.

How God Uncovered Secret Witchcraft

A few years later, a young woman who used to attend the same prayer meeting called me wanting deliverance. We got together, and she explained that she could not sing any longer. She used to sing in the church's choir, and even sang solos, but now she could no longer get her voice out, and she felt that there was a demon in her throat. When I started to cast out the demon, the Holy Spirit revealed to her the cause of her problem by bringing an incident to her mind. Once, when she was singing a solo at the church, she saw the leader of the prayer meeting coming down the aisle, looking for a seat. When the lady saw her singing at the altar, she turned around and left the church in a huff. Later on, a friend told her that the lady was relating that the young woman "*did not have any right to minister.*" I understood that she had been cursed by the lady, and that the name of the curse that gave the demon a right to enter was "No right to minister." I broke that curse in the name of Jesus, and Surprise! - I started to have deliverance also! It was then that I found out that the lady had also cursed me with the same curse: "No right to minister."

That lady is a respected Christian woman, the mother of a pastor. She has been conducting the prayer meeting for years, and she is invited to numerous churches to hold women's seminars. Women flock to her prayer meeting and think highly of her. Yet, in the spiritual world, she is a Charismatic Witch. Why? because she has a Jezebel spirit, that is compelling her to be domineering and to do anything to get her way. She was of the opinion that neither the other young woman nor I had a right to minister, so she prayed to cut off both our ministries. But through deliverance, the Holy Spirit uncovered her activity.

> *"For there is nothing covered that shall not be revealed; neither hid, that shall not be known. Therefore whatsoever ye have spoken in darkness shall be heard in the light; and that which ye have spoken in the ear in closets shall be proclaimed upon the housetops."*
>
> **Luke 12: 2,3**

Another Case of Charismatic Witchcraft

Some time ago, a lady called me for deliverance. I explained to her that I minister in the afternoon at the church certain days of the week. She said she worked full time and wanted me to come to her home in the evening. I told her I could not, and asked her if she could take a vacation day and come to receive ministry, but she said, "No, I can not get a vacation day off."

Then, I asked if she could take an afternoon off for personal business, and she again replied, "No, I cannot take an afternoon off for that, either. It has to be in the evening after work and at my house."

She was so adamant about the time and the place that I felt necessary to explain, that I was not part of the staff of the church and that I ministered deliverance on a voluntary basis. In other words, I explained, "Nobody pays me to do this." She told me she understood, so then I suggested that she read the deliverance manual which I had written, in order to prepare herself for deliverance. She read the manual, but I never heard from her again until about a year later, when she started to attend the deliverance classes I was teaching Saturday mornings.

Then, again she called me for deliverance and we had the exact same conversation as before. She wanted me to come to her house in the evening. In certain cases, I would make an exception, but not in this case. Because she was so demanding and so controlling, in trying to get me to I do it her way, I felt I should not comply with her demands. Instead, I asked about ministering to her during the class, since we have practical deliverance in the second half of the course. She said she did not want to have deliverance in front of the other students. I asked again about a vacation day again. She said her vacation was coming up the following month and therefore, we decided to wait till the following month and do it during her vacation.

In the interim, another girl called me seeking deliverance. She also worked full time and had just gotten her job, so she had not accrued any vacation time. Because she had just started working, she felt it was too early to be able to get any time off, so I asked her if she would mind coming to the class on Saturday morning. She said that would be fine. She did come and received deliverance, with the students helping in the ministry.

A few weeks later, I asked my other student when her vacation would start. To my surprise, she replied that it had come and gone. Why didn't you call me? I asked, and she replied "Don't worry and forget about it."

I was concerned about her attitude, so I called her that night to find the reason for her not calling me as we'd agreed. That conversation was upsetting. She complained that I had ministered to the other girl during the Saturday morning class, and denied having said that she did not want to be ministered to in front of the other students. She was extremely angry at me for not ministering to her at her home in the evening. Her tirade continued with no opportunity for me to put in a word.

Next morning when I awoke, I recalled the conversation with a sick feeling. Then the Lord spoke to me and said: "She has put a curse on you." I immediately broke the curse in the name of Jesus, and had some deliverance. Immediately after, I contacted someone who ministered to me about the same things and received still more deliverance.

I realized that the student had cursed me two weeks before. For two weeks I had been feeling very lethargic and sleepy. I had to take a nap in the morning and another in the afternoon, and was still not able to do much during the day. After this deliverance, all lethargy and sleepiness were gone, and I was as alert as usual.

Are You Under a Charismatic Witchcraft Curse?

When a Christian prays his or her own will (instead of God's will) regarding someone else, God will not hear the prayer, but Satan will take the opportunity and send a demon to fulfill the prayer in the other person. Thus, a self-willed, controlling Christian person could become a witch, not only in the eyes of God, but also in all the spiritual realm (just as conventional witches). Satan recognizes that person as a witch.

If more Christians were to become willing to receive deliverance, in addition to obtaining all kinds of freedom, they would surely uncover more Charismatic Witchcraft curses and bring them to the light. There is no telling how many men and women that are believed to be "good Christians," are praying these willful prayers and sending curses and demons against other Christians. In the natural, they seem to be Christians, have ministries, do good works, preach at churches, and prophesy. Even pastors set them forth as examples, and often financially assist their ministries. When the few Christians who do believe in deliverance, find out about their own witchcraft through deliverance as I did, they will not be believed if they try to expose the true spiritual condition of such individuals. The ministry and "good works" of the Charismatic Witches overwhelm the spiritual witness of the deliverance minister who will be regarded as a trouble-maker and a liar.

Pastors are the main target of the prayers of Charismatic Witches. Charismatic Witches want to charm their pastors into acting or thinking as *they* wish, and the way they do this, is through their "prayers." Pastors need deliverance from Charismatic Witchcraft curses!

"Pastors, WAKE UP!"

4

The Jezebellic Mother

A Jezebel spirit in a mother could influence the relationship with her children in different ways. One of the most common ways is through the spirit of control, which works under Jezebel.

A controlling mother wants her children to do, and think, what she wants them to do and think. The mother does not try to understand the needs of the children nor their point of view, she only wants them to do exactly as she says. As a child grows older it is natural that he or she begins being gradually independent in certain areas, which is a natural process of growing up.

The controlling mother comes against this process. At each stage of growth she wants to be the one to make the decisions which the child should be making by himself, or herself. The child feels the unnatural imposition of the mother's will, and reacts in either of two ways: one, the child submits to the mother and lets himself be dominated and controlled by the Jezebel spirit. Or, second, the child refuses to be controlled and the mother accuses him of being "rebellious." The child fights to maintain the independence that should be natural for his age and this provokes strife in the family. If the father has an Ahab spirit, he is already under the control of the woman, probably fears her and will not do anything for the child. The mother's attempt to control the mind of the child is a kind of brainwashing: every idea that the child comes up with is opposed, and the point of view of the mother has to be accepted. I am not talking about major moral issues. I am talking about trivial things. The mother's will must prevail. For instance, the mother takes her daughter to the store to buy a dress for her. Given the opportunity of selecting between two similar dresses of exactly the same price, when the daughter chooses one, the mother chooses the other and the daughter has to take it, or leave it.

The mother tries to control the child's thinking, opinions and taste. No matter the age of the child, the mother's thinking, opinion and taste has to prevail.

Old Age Companion

Sometimes a controlling mother will pick an easily dominated child to be the companion of her old age. In the case of an only child, even if the child does not allow himself or herself to be dominated, she will try by all means to get the child to remain single. She will try to persuade her child that the person he or she is interested in, is not good enough, is too old, is too poor, or is too anything. She influences and attempts to discourage the son or daughter from every relationship that might lead to marriage. If the child does marry, she will still be working, trying to break up the marriage.

A Sad Story

In the small town where I grew up, there was a widow who had two sons and a daughter. The sons got married over the objections of the mother. The daughter, a teacher, also had a boyfriend. The mother was violently opposed to the relationship.

In that sleepy old town, the houses have front porches which edge on the sidewalk. The custom was for girls to bring a rocking chair out to the porch at sundown, and for the boy to casually stroll by and stop, on the sidewalk side wrought iron railing of the porch, to visit with the girl. When the relationship became a little more serious, the boy would come every evening to visit in this fashion, until the time that the boy was ready to talk to the parents of the girl. Then, the boy would be allowed to visit in the living room, under the supervision of one of her parents, usually the mother.

The widow's daughter was being visited by the boy on the porch. He came by every night. They grew older, but still the mother opposed the relationship. They decided that they would wait to get married until after the old woman passed away. The couple kept growing older and year after year, every night, he came to visit his beloved, on the other side of the railing, bearing a little love gift of chocolates or candies. They could not even go to the movies or the park, for fear that the mother would have a heart attack because of her age. The old woman lived a long time, so long, in fact, that the suitor of her daughter died of old age, before the old woman died! This a true story and I know it because one of my aunts married one of the sons of that widow. What a sad story! Score one point for Jezebel.

Adios, Mama's Boy!

The spirits of control which work under Jezebel fashion Mama's Boys. Mama's Boys are good boys who obey their Jezebellic mothers as long as they live. As in the previous story, the mother wants the son for herself, and attains her goal through brainwashing, persuasion, and manipulation.

As a University of Havana student living in Havana, Cuba, with my parents, I had a young couple as neighbors who had recently moved to a nearby house. They had a friend whom they wanted me to meet. Their friend had already graduated. He had an engineering degree from a good university in the United States, and he had a very good job in Havana with one of the big U.S. oil companies. He was about twenty-eight years old and single. Since I was about to become a graduate architect, they wanted us to meet. "But", they warned me, "Be careful. He is a Mama's Boy."

They tried to invite him to dinner and he finally told them that he must always have dinner with his mother. So they had him over in the afternoon and asked me to come. I arrived and met him, and after some conversation, the young couple asked him to stay for dinner. He obviously wanted to stay but seemed concerned. Finally he announced that he would have to call his mother — not in order to politely advise her that he would be having dinner with friends — but to ask her permission. The mother told him no, and in fact, she must also have told him to get home, because he left right away.

He called me once or twice after that. Soon after it was his birthday, and he called to invite me to the movies in the afternoon. "To celebrate my birthday," he said. As the time for our date was approaching, my neighbors were astonished that their friend had dared invite me to the movies. They were in doubt that it would ever happen.

Sure enough, thirty minutes before the time that he said he would be at my home, he called. He could not take me to the movies. He had told his mother of his plans, and she had a fit. He had to take her to the movies instead. By themselves. Good-Bye, Mama's Boy!

Old Maids and Old Bachelors

Not all people who remain single do so as a result of a Jezebellic mother. I would say that only half of them are. Perhaps in the "olden" times it was more prevalent. When I was younger, I knew families where the mother ruled both sons and daughters with an iron hand, and had already broken up relationships that could have led to marriages.

The Spirit of Selfishness

Jezebel feels that she is the center of the universe. One of the facets of Jezebel is selfishness. Although selfishness is found both in men and women, when it is found in a woman it is most probably working under Jezebel.

CHARACTERISTICS:
1- The number one characteristic of a selfish person is that he/she is incapable of recognizing that he/she is selfish. A selfish person is blind to his/her selfishness. Some other sins are readily recognized and confessed: "I am fearful." "I am an adulterer." "I have hate in my heart." In my experience as a deliverance minister, I have never yet heard anyone recognize and confess to being selfish. On the contrary, when selfishness is pointed out to the selfish Christian, there will be a vehement denial of it. They are being sincere because they truly cannot believe that they are selfish.

2- They love to talk about themselves down to the last detail. What they ate (dish by dish), how they digested it, how they slept, what dreams they had, how their health is, what they are feeling, what medicines they are taking, what the doctor told them. When they call a friend, if they are polite they will ask their friend: "How are you?" But they are not interested in hearing the answer. They immediately start talking about themselves. They hardly talk about anything else.

3- When they call a friend, they do not ask the friend if he/she is busy at the moment. They do not care. They just charge on with their conversation. If the friend is having dinner at the moment, or giving the baby a bath, too bad. What they have to say is more important.

4- When they want something from a friend, they want it right away. They want the friend to drop what he/she is doing to attend to their need. If the friend does not, they feel offended.

5- They do not have any regard for other people's time. They will arrive late for appointments. It does not bother them that there are people waiting for them. What makes them late? Whatever comes up that interests them. The others can wait.

Selfish people take their pleasure first. They are "Number One." They believe that the rest of humanity is there to serve them. They are people-users.

The Consequences of Selfishness

Extremely selfish Christians seem to always have problems. Maybe it is because they magnify their own problems, this is the nature of selfishness. In my experience, selfish Christians seem to need deliverance often. It seems that they never reach a point of peace in their lives. As long as the person is selfish, it is going to be difficult for that person to be free.

There are strong warnings in the Bible against selfishness. If these warnings are not heeded, the demons have a legal right to enter and do their evil work.

Therefore all things whatsoever you would that men should do to you, do ye even so to them: for this is the law and the prophets.
Matthew 7: 12

Master, which is the great commandment in the law? Jesus said unto him, Thou shalt love the Lord thy God with all thy heart, and with all thy soul, and with all thy mind. This is the first and great commandment. And the second is like unto it, Thou shalt love thy neighbor as thyself. On these two commandments hang all the law and the prophets.
Matthew 22: 36-40

For all the law is fulfilled in one word, even this: Thou shalt love thy neighbor as thyself.
Galatians 5: 14

If ye fulfill the royal law according to the scripture, Thou shalt love thy neighbor as thyself, **ye do well.**
James 2: 8

...if there be any other commandment, it is briefly comprehended in this saying, namely, Thou shalt love thy neighbor as thyself.
Romans 13: 9

The Selfish Jezebellic Mother

The selfish jezebellic mother does not want to have children, she does not want to be bothered with them, they cramp her style. Since her needs and desires come first, the care and mothering of children is overwhelming to her. She does not want to give of herself. What is the first reaction of a selfish, Jezebellic woman when she is told she is pregnant? What attitude does a selfish, Jezebellic woman take with her own children?

Abortion. The idea of abortion is the first result of the Jezebellic selfishness.

Child Abuse. Child abuse is a natural reaction of the selfish Jezebellic mother. She did not want children to start with. If she has them, she resents them. The demands of child rearing makes her resent the children even more. This resentment, combined with the spirit of control leads her to abuse the children physically, mentally and emotionally. This kind of mother will reach the point of hating her children, a feeling that most mothers would try to conceal. Once the children are grown and out of her care, the resentment against them is still there. This kind of mother sometimes copes by **neglecting** the children. Jezebel is identified with Isis and Ceres, who are connected to Moloch, the pagan god to whom children were sacrificed.

SPIRITS OF SELFISHNESS:
Selfishnesss, egoism, egolatry, egotism, egomania, number one, focal point, center of attention, center

38

of attraction, center of the universe, self, adoration of self, idolatry of self, people user, big "me" little "you," "I deserve everything."

SPIRITS OF CHILD ABUSE:
Provocation, destruction of sons (and daughters), disrespect of sons (and daughters), belittlement of sons (and daughters), humiliation of sons (and daughters) hatred of sons (and daughters), jealousy of sons (and daughters), physical child abuse, mental child abuse, verbal child abuse, emotional child abuse, psychological child abuse, negligence of sons (and daughters) abortion, murder, Moloch.

The Competitive Spirit, or Spirit of Competition.

A competitive spirit is promoted in sports as each athlete tries to better him/herself during practice and at each event. Everyone tries to develop a sense of being a good sport, a good winner, a good loser. We try to be the best we can be.

There is nothing wrong with this. We should strive to be the best, the most productive, or the most creative that we can be. We should strive to use the talents that God has given us to the fullest.

However, a sick attitude of competition indicates an evil spirit that is one of Jezebel's attendants. I have encountered this demon in everyday situations and have learned to recognize it after several experiences.

Competing When There Is No Competition:

Once I invited a woman friend from church to my home after a service. We each came in our own car, and were going on the same street at approximately the same speed.

Approaching our house, there was a traffic light where we would turn left. However, the timing of the light was such that we sat in the left turn lane waiting for the light to turn green seemingly forever, while the other lanes had the green light for quite a long time. Because of this delay, my husband and I decided it was best to continue straight and turn left at the next street where there was no traffic light.

It was only helpful to get in the left turn lane, if we were able to get to that traffic light at the right time, when the light was about to change. Most often, we seemed to get there at the wrong time. That day, my friend got in the left turn lane and I continued straight to the next street as I usually did. I was driving at my regular speed and when I arrived at my driveway, my friend was already out of her car waiting for me.

When I got out, I was stunned by my friend's behavior. She had a weird expression on her face, and told me with cackling laughter that she had beaten me to my house. She was full of glee and kept repeating "I beat you, I beat you." I was shocked, since I had never seen her act that way.

Finally all I could say to her was that I did not know that we were racing! I have never forgotten that incident. She was a grown mature woman, definitely past the age of drag racing.

I later realized that her attitude was caused by the competitive demon manifesting in her.

The competitive, or competition, demon will make a person argumentative and want to have the last word. It will make the person hold onto an erroneous idea and maintain it, even after he/she finds out that it is not correct. It will make the person state that their choices in life are the best ones, even about trivial, unimportant things.

I once worked with a Christian lady, who liked to talk about what restaurants she and her husband went to for each different kind of food. If I would mention the restaurant that my husband and I went to for that kind of food, her expression would change to one of extreme concern. She would say "Oh, no!" in dismay, and then change to an air of superiority in telling me, "We go to such and such restaurant." I finally realized that I had entered a "restaurant competition" with her and that I better avoid the subject.

If I were to have had the same demon, we would have been involved in endless arguments. Strife, argument, dispute, disagreement and fighting are demons which help the demon of competition.

Living or working with a person that has this demon leads to a lot of arguments. It also makes the people who have it, behave in silly ways. Would you believe trying to getting to a door first?

Getting to the door first!

I have experienced this unusual problem with two different women in two different situations. I am writing about this silly happening to help you to discern this spirit. Sometimes we are in situations that make us wonder what is going on, and not until later, when we gather more knowledge about deliverance and the spirit world, are we able to discern the demons that were at work in those previous situations.

I barely knew the one lady who called me. I knew she was Christian and moved in deliverance circles. She was complaining about a friend that wouldn't take her along when she went to minister deliverance. She complained to me, "How would she ever be able to learn anything?"

I told her that I would take her with me the next time I ministered. The time soon came, and I drove with her to the house of one of my friends who wanted to receive ministry.

As I got out of the car, this lady (also a mature lady, who'd gotten to an age that she could not be very fast on her feet) maneuvered and hurried ahead, almost shoving me aside, as I was heading for the door. I was puzzled by this behavior, since she did not know the lady of the house, who would be opening the door.

Once inside, she tried to take control of the deliverance ministry and managed to be the center of attention. No wonder the other minister did not want her joining her party!

The second instance in which I encountered this situation was in a business situation. The same lady of the restaurants story had to get to all the doors first when we were calling on prospective clients. Later I realized that it was the spirit of competition working in her.

Characteristics of the Demon of Competition:
> I am the best.
> I win.
> What I think is the way it is.
> What I say is the way it is.
> I have the last word.
> I am more important.
> My choices are the best.
> I go in first.
> I know better.

Demons often found helping the demon of Competition:
> Argument, strife, contention, bickering, disagreement, debate, altercation, quarreling, discussion, controvert, conflict, dissension, friction, fighting, battle, clash, combat, dispute, assert, maintain, insist.

5

The Names of
Ahab and
Jezebel
In Antiquity

A Revelation

Recently, while casting a Jezebel demon out of a young Christian woman, the Holy Spirit told me: *"Jezebel has additional names: one is Isis, another is Ishtar..."* I immediately commanded the Jezebel demon to tell me her other names. Reluctantly, and with a broken voice, she answered: *"Ishtar..."*

Then I understood that the demon behind all the goddesses of antiquity was the demon that now calls herself Jezebel. It stands to reason then, that the counterpart of Jezebel, Ahab, is Baal and all the other gods of antiquity. After this revelation, I have found it much easier to cast Jezebel out by calling by all her names and also casting those demons out.

The Feminist Movement and the Goddesses

When the feminist movement started, I was working as a female Architect in a male environment. Because I was not a man, I was paid much less salary. The Architectural firm I worked for landed a new project and were too busy for it. I knew I was capable of handling that project and thought they would give it to me. Instead, they hired a recent male graduate, sat him next to me, gave him the project and told me that since I had the experience, I would be helping him to do everything that he did not know how to do! I was very disappointed and felt discriminated against for being a woman.

Previously, the Department of Labor had sent a man to investigate our company. It seemed that someone had informed them that I was underpaid. He interviewed me, and sometime later the secretary came to my drafting table with a check for me that I was supposed to keep secret. They also raised my salary a little bit. It appeared that they had to compensate me for the under-payment, but I was never paid while in that office, the same rate that the men doing the same kind of work I was doing were paid.

So when the feminist movement started, I was for it. Perhaps the custom of paying women less for the same job was what started the whole movement. Paying women less for the same job, just because they are women, is still an injustice being perpetuated today.

Soon enough I realized that something was not right with the women's movement and I did not join. Now, I know that what I was perceiving was that Jezebel had taken control of it.

Robert H. Bork, in his book *Slouching Toward Gomorrah* (Regan Books\Harper Collins Books) says: "Diane Knippers, president of the Institute on Religion and Democracy, reports than in Beijing the feminists built a shrine to the goddesses out of red ribbons in the shape of a Christmas tree decorated with paper dolls representing the goddesses. Women were invited to make and add their own goddesses. The organization headed by Bella Abzug held daily programs, each one dedicated to a different goddess: **Songi, Athena, Tara, Pasowee, Ishtar, Ixmucane, Aditi** and **Nashe.**

Names of Pagan Goddesses and Their Identity

The following is a list of the names of pagan goddesses and their consorts. This list will help with deliverance of the Jezebel and Ahab demons. There might be more ancient goddesses related to Jezebel, than shown in the list. Also, not all of these will be found in each deliverance case that you encounter.

Ashera— This is the Hebrew rendering of Asherat, the leading goddess of the Phoenician Canaanites and consort of the head of their pantheon. She represented the

female principle in the fertility cult. During the reign of king Ahab, his queen, Jezebel of Tyre, who had brought her worship of the Tyrian gods to her adopted land, secured official status for the "four hundred and fifty prophets of Baal and four hundred prophets of Ashera"(I Kings 18:19) This led to the dramatic confrontation with Elijah on mount Carmel. King Josiah destroyed the Ashera idol in Jerusalem.
(*Who is Who in the Bible*, Bonanza Books)

> *Now therefore send, and gather to me all Israel unto mount Carmel, and the prophets of Baal four hundred and fifty, and the prophets of the groves four hundred, which eat at Jezebel's table.*
>
> ***1 Kings 18:19***

Ashtaroth— This is the plural Hebrew form for the Canaanite goddess Astarte, one of the dominant female deities of fertility. From the numerous "Astarte" plaques discovered in archeological excavations, this goddess was usually represented naked. The name is often used as a general term for female deities of Canaan. Also called **Astoreth.** (*Who is Who in the Bible*, Bonanza Books)

Ashera, plural, Asherim— Where the King James version of the Bible says "groves", it means Asherim. This was the name of a sensual Canaanite goddess also called **Anath, Ashtoreth or Astarte, the Assyrian Ishtar**. Her symbol was the stem of a tree deprived of its boughs, and rudely shaped into an image, and planted in the ground. Such religious symbols, "groves" are frequently alluded in scripture. (Exodus 34:13, Judges 6:25, etc.)

These images are sometimes made out of silver or of carved stone (2 Kings 21:7) "The graven image of Ashera."

(*Today's Dictionary of the Bible*, Guideposts)

But you shall destroy their altars, break their images, and cut down their groves.

Exodus 34: 13

And it came to pass the same night, that the Lord said unto him, Take thy father's young bullock, even the second bullock of seven years old, and throw down the altar of Baal that thy father hath, and cut down the grove that is by it.

Judges 6:25

And he set a graven image of the grove that he had made in the house, of which the Lord said to David, and to Solomon his son, In this house, and in Jerusalem, which I have chosen out of all tribes of Israel, will I put my name forever.

2 Kings 21:7

Ashera, or Athirat— Ancient Canaanite goddess known widely in the Ancient Near East. In the Ras Shamra texts she is portrayed as consort of the god El, and mother of the gods....

(*Larousse Dictionary of beliefs and Religions*)

Ashtoreth— The moon goddess of the Phoenicians, representing the passive principle in nature, their principal female deity, frequently associated with the name of Baal, the chief male deity (Judges 10:6, I Samuel 7:4, 12:10).

These names often occur in the plural (Ashtaroth, **Baalim**) probably as indicating either different statues or different modifications of the deities. This deity is spoken of as **Ashtoreth of the Sidonians**. She was the Ishtar of the Assyrians and the Astarte of the Greeks. (I Kings 11:5, II Kings 23:13, Jeremiah 44:17) There was a temple of this goddess among the Philistines in the time of Saul (I Samuel 31:10). Under the name of **Ishtar**, she was one of the great deities of the Assyrians. The Phoenicians called her **Astarte**.

Solomon introduced the worship of this idol (I Kings 18:19). It was called **"The Queen of Heaven"** (Jer. 44:25)
(*Today's Dictionary of the Bible*, Guideposts)

> *And the children of Israel did evil again in the sight of the Lord, and served Baalim, and Ashtaroth, and the gods of Syria, and the gods of Zidon, and the gods of Moab, and the gods of the children of Ammon, and the gods of the Philistines, and forsook the Lord, and served not Him.*
>
> ***Judges 10:6***

> *Then the children of Israel did put away Baalim and Ashtaroth and served the Lord only.*
>
> ***1 Samuel 7:4***

> *And they cried unto the Lord, and said, We have sinned, because we have forsaken the Lord, and have served Baalim and Ashtaroth: but now deliver us out of the hand of our enemies, and we will serve thee.*
>
> ***1 Samuel 12:10***

For Solomon went after Ashtoreth the goddess of the Zidonians, and after Milcom the abomination of the Ammonites.

1 Kings 11:5

And the high places that were before Jerusalem, which were on the right hand of the mount of corruption, which Solomon the king of Israel had builded for Ashtoreth the abomination of the Zidonians, and for Chemosh the abomination of the Moabites, and for Milcom the abomination of the children of Ammon, did the king defile.

2 Kings 23:13

But we will certainly do whatsoever thing goeth forth out of our own mouth, to burn incense to the queen of heaven, and to pour out drink offerings unto her, as we have done, we, and our fathers, our kings, and our princes, in the cities of Judah, and in the streets of Jerusalem; for then had we plenty of victuals, and were well, and saw no evil.

Jeremiah 44:17

And they put his armour in the house of Ashtaroth: and they fastened his body to the wall of Beth-shan.

1 Samuel 31:10

Thus saith the Lord of hosts, the God of Israel, saying: Ye and your wives have both spoken with your mouths, and fulfilled with your hand, saying, We will surely perform our vows that we have vowed, to burn incense to the queen of heaven, and to pour out drink offerings unto her: ye will surely accomplish your vows, and surely perform your vows.

Jeremiah 44:25

Ashtoreth— (Plural, Ashtaroth) A goddess of the Phoenicians and Canaanites; also called **Astarte**, and in Babilonia, **Ishtar**. She was a goddess of sexual love. maternity and fertility. Her worship was early established at Sidon and was popular east of the Jordan in the days of Abraham. As early as the time of the judges it had spread to the Hebrews (Judges 2:13, 10:6). Solomon in his old age gave it support (I Kings 11: 5, II Kings 23:13).

Prophets strove earnestly and constantly to wipe out the worship of her, which suggests that she had much appeal to peoples dependent on the fertility of soil and flock.

(*20th Century Bible Dictionary*, Abingdon)

And they forsook the Lord, and served Baal and Ashtaroth

Judges 2:13

And the children of Israel did evil again in the sight of the Lord, and served Baalim, and Ashtaroth,and the gods of Syria, and the gods of Zidon, and the gods of Moab, and the gods of the children of Ammon, and the gods of the Philistines, and forsook the Lord, and served not him.

Judges 10:6

For Solomon went after Ashtoreth the goddess of the Zidonians, and after Milcom the abomination of the Ammonites.

1 Kings 11:5

*And the high places that were before Jerusalem,
which were on the right hand of the mount of corruption, which Solomon the king of Israel had
builded for Ashtoreth the abomination of the
Zidonians, and for Chemosh the abomination of the
Moabites, and for Milcom the abomination of the
children of Ammon, did the king defile.*

2 Kings 23:13

Ishtar— A Semite goddess worshipped in Phoenicia,
Canaan, Assyria and Babylonia. Her name is spelled in
various ways: **Ashtoreth, Astarte, Ashtarte** (In the
Amarna letters), **Ishtar** (in Babilonia) etc. The name and
cult of the goddess were derived from Babilonia, where
she was the goddess of love and war. Prostitution was
practiced in her name by bands of men and women. In
Assyria the war like side of the goddess was stressed. In
Canaan her warlike attributes were dropped, and she
became a moon goddess and the consort of Baal. The
Philistines worshipped her and built a temple for her at
Ascalon. As early as the times of Judges her cult had
spread to the Hebrews (Judges 2:13, 10:6) Solomon sup-
ported her worship (I Kings 11:3, II Kings 23:13) and
the Hebrew women in Jeremiah's day gave her a high
place in their worship.
(*The New Compact Bible Dictionary*, Pillar Books)

*And he had seven hundred wives, princesses, and
three hundred concubines; and his wives turned
away his heart.*

1 Kings 11:3

This presentation of the meaning of the name Astarte has been condensed from *The Two Babylons*, Hislop, Loizeaux Brothers, Inc.

Semiramis— under the name of **Astarte**, was worshipped not only as an incarnation of the Spirit of God, but as the mother of mankind. The name Astarte has reference to her as being **Rhea or Cybele**, the tower bearing goddess. "The first", as Ovid says, "that made towers in cities." In Syria she was represented standing on a lion crowned with towers. She was queen of Babylon. **Ash-Toreth**, same as **Ash-Turit** is "the woman that made the encompassing wall." The Greek goddess **Diana** at Ephesus wore a turreted crown on her head, and was identified with Semiramis. She was the goddess of fortifications, and people would go to her when they dreaded an attack on their city.

She was called "**the mother of the gods**." For a time her emblem was a dove. She was celebrated as the originator of some of the arts and sciences. The Grecian **Minerva**, also called **Athena**, is a synonym for **Beltis**, the well known name of the Assyrian goddess. Minerva was known as the "goddess of wisdom", the inventress of arts and sciences. The name Astarte also means "the maker of investigations." It was **Asterie**, the wife of **Perseus** the Assyrian, founder of Mysteries. Asterie was represented as the daughter of **Bel**. **Astrea** was the goddess of justice, identified with the heavenly virgin **Themis**, "the perfect one." Themis and Astrea are sometimes found to be the same, both are "goddess of justice." In some cultures, they tried to identify her as the Holy Spirit. Some said that she was in Noah's Ark as spirit, and thence Semiramis was worshipped as the dove.

As **Baal**, "lord of heaven" had the sun as his emblem, so she, **Beltis,** "queen of heaven" had the moon. They identified her with Eve, because they thought of her as the mother of the human race. Both the title **Aphrodite** and **Mylitta** are attributed to her. Mylitta means "the **mediatrix**" (a woman mediator). **Melitza** and **Melissa,** meaning sweet, is a common name for **Cybele** or **Astarte**, **Queen of Heaven**, which is also the title for **Semiramis**. Melissa is said to have been the mother of **Phoroneus**, "The first that reigned." During his reign mankind dispersed and acquired other languages, so Phoroneus is **Nimrod**, who came to be worshipped as **Nin**, the son of his own wife. **Melitta** then is **Mylitta,** the well known name of the Babylonian **Venus**, and her name is the mediatrix. Another name given to her is **Archia**, which means "spiritual" (In Egyptian, "Rkh", in Caldee, "Arkh."

Diana— Roman goddess, associated with the moon, fertility and hunting. She was considered to be equivalent with the Greek **Artemis,** whose cult was primarily at Ephesus, hence the cult of "Diana of the Ephesians," who was a fertility goddess.
(*Larousse Dictionary of Beliefs and Religions*)

Anahita— Prominent female divinity known in the Zoroastrian tradition as **Ardvi Sura Anahita,** "the moist, mighty pure one"...the cult of the latter divinity, perhaps inspired by the goddess **Ishtar** in neighboring Babylonia, appears to be very popular in western Iran when Zoroastrianism first became prominent there...the divinity is

primarily associated with water, with prosperity and with women's affairs....
(*Larousse Dictionary of Beliefs and Religions*)

Anat or **Anath**— Canaanite goddess of love and war, sister and probably consort of Baal. In the Ras Shamra text Anat is described by the epithet "virgin" and presented as a violent helper of Baal....Anat became known in Egypt as the consort of **Baal-Sutekh,** and was chosen as personal patron by the Pharaoh Rameses II ....In the Hellenistic period she was fused with the goddess Astarte and worshiped as **Atargatis,** the "Syrian goddess."
(*Larousse Dictionary of Beliefs and Religions*)

Baal— The chief god of the Canaanites. Baal was worshipped as the god of the elements who brought rain and made the ground fruitful, and sometimes as the god of war. Temples to Baal were established on high places throughout Israel and many of the Children of Israel worshipped there from the days of the Judges. In the reign of King Ahab, Baal worship became the court religion and led to Elijah's confrontation with the prophets of Baal on Mount Carmel. The worshippers of Baal were later massacred by King Jehu but the influence of Baal remained throughout the period of the first Temple and brought about frequent strictures by the prophets of Israel and Judah. **Bel, Belus, Baalim and Merodach** were alternative names for **Baal** and many places were named in honor of Baal.
(*Who is Who in the Bible*, Bonanza Books)

Baal-Berith— (Heb. "lord of the covenant") 12 Cen-

tury B.C. The Canaanite god of Sechem in the time of Abimelech, the rebellious son of Gideon the Judge. He was also called **El-Berith.** (Judges 8:33; 9:4)
(*Who is Who in the Bible*, Bonanza Books)

> *And it came to pass, as soon as Gideon was dead, that the children of Israel turned again, and went a-whoring after Baalim, and made Baal-Berith their god.* **Judges 8:33**

> *And they gave him three score and ten pieces of silver out of the house of Baal-Berith, wherwith Abimelech hired vain and light persons, which followed him.* **Judges 9:4**

Baal-Zebub— (Heb. "lord of the flies") The name for the local god of the Philistine city of Ekron. When King Ahaziah lay sick and sent messengers to find out of this deity whether he would recover, they were waylaid by the angry prophet Elijah who upbraided them with the words: "Is because there is no God in Israel to inquire of his word?" (2 Kings 1:16) Elijah then foretold the King's death (2 Kings 1: 2,3,6,16)
(*Who is Who in the Bible,* Bonanza Books)

> *And he said unto him, Thus saith the Lord, Forasmuch as thou hast sent messengers to inquire of Baal-Zebub the god of Ekron, is it not because there is no God in Israel to inquire of his word? Therefore thou shalt not come down off that bed on which thou art gone up, but shalt surely die.* **2 Kings 1:16**

And Ahaziah fell down through a lattice is his upper chamber that was in Samaria, and was sick; and he sent messengers, and said unto them, Go, inquire of Baal-Zebub the god of Ekron whether I shall recover of this disease. But the angel of the Lord said to Elijah the Tishbite, Arise, go up to meet the messengers of the king of Samaria, and say unto them, Is it not because there is not a God in Israel, that ye go to inquire of Baal-Zebub the god of Ekron?

2 Kings 1:2,3

And They said unto him, There came a man up to meet us, and said unto us, Go, turn again unto the king that sent you, and say unto him, Thus saith the Lord, Is it not because there is not a God in Israel, that thou sendest to inquire of Baal-Zebub the god of Ekron? Therefore thou shalt not come down from that bed on which thou art gone up, but shalt surely die

2 Kings 1:6

The following is from *The Two Babylons* by the Rev. Alexander Hislop:

Isis— In the Greek mythology **Kronos** and **Rhea** are commonly brother and sister. **Ninus** and **Semiramis**, according to history, are not represented as standing in any such relation to one another; but this is no objection to the real identity of **Ninus** and **Kronus**, for first, the relation of the divinities, in most countries, are peculiarly conflicting. **Osiris**, in Egypt, is represented at different times, not only as the son and husband of **Isis**, but also as her father and brother (*Bunsen*, Vol 1, p. 438).

It is admitted that the secret system of Free Masonry was originally founded on the mysteries of the Egyptian **Isis,** the goddess mother-wife of **Osiris.**

The Egyptian Isis, the sister-wife of Osiris, is in like manner represented, as we have seen, as "lamenting for her brother Osiris" (**Tammuz,** Ezekiel 8:14)

The ordinary way in which the favorite Egyptian divinity Osiris was mystically represented was under the form of a young bull or calf–the calf **Apis**–from which the golden calf of the Israelites was borrowed. "The hidden one," Apis, being only another name for **Saturn.**

Osiris, in Greece, is identified with the Greek **Dionysus, Bacchus** or **Iacchus**. (Note that Bacchus has to do with drunkenness) All of them are also identified with **Nimrod**.

In Egypt, the fair Horus, the son of the black Osiris, who was the favorite object of worship in the arms of the goddess Isis, was said to have been born in consequence of a connection, on the part of the goddess, with Osiris after his death.

In Egypt, the son of **Isis,** the Egyptian title for **queen of heaven**, was born at this very time, "about the time of winter solstice"

Although the god that Isis or **Ceres** brought forth, and who was offered to her under the symbol of the wafer or thin round cake as the "bread of life" was in reality the fierce, scorching sun, or terrible **Moloch ...** (Jeremiah 7:18, Leviticus 18:21, 20: 2-5, 1 Kings 11:7, 2 Kings 23:10, Jer. 32:35)

Then he brought me to the door of the gate of the Lord's house which was toward the north; and be-

58

hold, there sat women weeping for Tammuz.

Ezekiel 8:14

The children gather wood, and the fathers kindle the fire, and the women knead their dough, to make cakes to the queen of heaven, and to pour out drink offerings unto other gods, that they make provoke me to anger.

Jeremiah 7:18

And thou shalt not let any of thy seed pass through the fire to Molech, neither shalt thou profane the name of thy God; I am the Lord

Leviticus 18:21

Again, thou shalt say to the children of Israel, Whosoever he be of the children of Israel, or of the strangers that sojourn in Israel, that giveth any of his seed unto Molech; he shall surely be put to death: the people of the land shall stone him with stones. And I will set my face against that man, and will cut him off from among his people; because he hath given of his seed unto Molech, to defile my sanctuary, and to profane my holy name.   And if the people of the land do any ways hide their eyes from the man, when he giveth of his seed unto Molech, and kill him not: Then I will set my face against that man, and against his family, and will cut him off, and all that go a- whoring after him, to commit whoredom with Molech, from among their people.

Leviticus 20: 2-5

Then did Salomon build an high place for Chemosh.

abomination of Moab, in the hill that is before Jerusalem, and for Molech, the abomination of the children of Ammon.

1 Kings 11:7

And he defiled Topheth, which is in the valley of the children of Hinnom, that no man might make his son or his daughter to pass through the fire to Molech.

2 Kings 23:10

And they built the high places of Baal, which are in the valley of Hinnom, to cause their sons and their daughters to pass through the fire unto Molech; which I commanded them not, neither came it into my mind, that they should do this abomination, to cause Judah to sin.

Jeremiah 32:35

Shing Moo - The name Shing Moo, applied by the Chinese to their **"Holy Mother"** compares with another name for the same goddess in another province of China, strongly favors the conclusion that Shing Moo is just a synonym for one of the well-known names of the goddess-mother of Babylon.

(The above excerpts for Isis, Osiris and Shing Moo are from *The Two Babylons*, Rev. Alexander Hislop, Loizeaux Brothers, Inc. pages 31, 43, 44, 45, 46, 69, 93, 294.)

Please note that the word "Easter" is derived from

Ishtar. One of the attributes of the goddess was fertility. Fertility is naturally celebrated in spring. This is the reason for the eggs and the bunnies, they are a sign of fertility. Our Christian celebration of the resurrection of Jesus Christ should be called Resurrection, not Easter.

After studying the names of the goddesses of antiquity and what they stood for, I got an impression that Jezebel is also an impostor for Mary, the mother of Jesus. The title "Queen of Heaven" and "Mediatrix" which is mediator or intercessor, lead to this. **Sati**, the wife of **Shiva** (Main Hindu God) was seen by Shiva dressed in white and holding a rosary in her hands. The Ephesian **Diana** had a rosary. (*The Two Babylons*, Rev. Alexander Hislop)

Back to Mama's Boy

Behind pagan images of gods and goddesses of antiquity there was a spirit operating supernatural feats. Behind several of the goddesses of antiquity was the spirit that now calls herself Jezebel. This is the spirit that was behind Semiramis. Semiramis was called "Queen of Heaven," and also was represented and worshipped as a dove.

The following is from *The Two Babylons*, by Rev. Alexander Hislop, Chapter II, Section II:
"The Babylonians in their popular religion supremely worshipped a goddess mother and son, who was represented in pictures and in images as an infant and child in his mother's arms. From Babylon this worship of the

mother and child spread to the ends of the earth. In Egypt, the worship was under the name of **Isis** and **Osiris**. In India, even to this day, is **Isi** and **Iswara**, in Asia as **Cybele** and **Dedius**, in pagan Rome as **Fortuna** and **Jupiter-puer** or **Jupiter** the boy, in Greece as **Ceres** the **Great Mother** with the babe at her breast or as **Irene,** the goddess of peace with the boy **Plutus** in her arms, and in Tibet, in China and Japan, the Jesuit missionaries were astonished to find the counterpart of **Madonna** and her child as devoutly worshipped as in Papal Rome itself; **Shing-Moo**, the **Holy Mother** in China being represented with a child in her arms and a *glory* around her, exactly as if a Roman Catholic artist had been employed to set her up."

The original Babylonian goddess was **Semiramis**, and her son **Tammuz**, also known as **Bacchus** the "lamented one."

The following is from *The Two Babylons* by Rev. Alexander Hislop, Chapter II, Sub-section I:

"The lamented one, exhibited and adored as a little child in his mother's arms, seems, in point of fact, to have been the husband of **Semiramis**, whose name, **Ninus,** by which he is commonly known in classical history, literally signified "The Son"........Ninus is sometimes called the husband and sometimes the son of Semiramis."

The word Ninus has come to the Spanish language as Niño, which means small boy. In some families the younger boy continues being called "El Niño" even when he is an adult. Catholics worship "El Niño Jesus," for-

62

getting that Jesus was a child for only a short time, as all of us were, and that He grew to adulthood. The famous Pacific ocean current called "El Niño" was originally identified by the Peruvians as "El Niño Jesus"

Conclusion: Mama's Boy

The confusion in the relationship between the mother and son who also was the husband, is the character of the goddess-demon that is now known as Jezebel. This explains why a Jezebellian mother will raise a "Mama's Boy." She wants the son all for herself, she does not want to share him with another woman. The son eventually takes the place of a husband in her life.

The following Scriptures refer to the worship of Semiramis:

*Seest thou not what they do in the cities of Judah and in the streets of Jerusalem? The children gather wood and the fathers kindle the fire, and the women knead their dough to make cakes to the **queen of heaven**, and to pour out drink offerings unto other gods, that they may provoke me to anger.*
Jeremiah 7: 17,18

*He said also unto me, Turn thee yet again, and thou shalt see greater abominations that they do. Then he brought me to the door of the gate of the Lord's house which was toward the north; and behold, there sat women weeping for **Tammuz** .*
Ezekiel 8: 13,14

The Wiccan Goddesses

William Schonoebelen in his book "Wicca" (*Chick Publications*, P.O. Box 662, Chino CA 91708-0662) makes mention of the following goddesses that are invoked or otherwise worshipped in Wiccan rites:

Artemis, Astarte, Athene, Dione, Melusine, Aphrodite, Cerridwen, Dana, Arianrhod, Isis, Bride. These names are Greek, Egyptian, Irish, Welsh and French. He also mentions **"Changing Woman"** (American Indian), **Shakti** (Hindu), **Semiramis,** the **"Immaculately Conceived" Blessed Virgin Mary**, and **Aida Odeo** (Obeah goddess)

6

Casting out
Ahab
And Jezebel

The Characteristics of Jezebel

Demanding, possessive, controlling, dominating, manipulative, scheming, taking charge of things, authoritarian, argumentative, jealous, wants to do things her way, gossipy, proud, arrogant, haughty, with excess of makeup, excess of jewelry, practicing witchcraft or charismatic witchcraft, demands to be the center of attention, selfish, sensual, manipulates or controls through sex, unsubmissive, tyrannical, harsh with her children, egoist or selfish, self-centered. Likes to put down people, mainly her husband and children.

Not all these characteristics will appear in one woman at the same time, although, they could be latent or veiled.

It easy to tell that a woman has a strong Jezebel if she has an excess of makeup, false lashes, wears too much jewelry, is arrogant and likes to be the center of attention. However, a woman with no make up and modestly dressed could be just as manipulative or controlling because of a Jezebel spirit. Each of the above characteristics is a demon that works under Jezebel. Jezebel is a demon of high rank, and has told me several times that she is a prince or principality.

Characteristics of Ahab

Weak, childish, a brat, pouts, careless, subject to temper tantrums, is spoiled, relinquishes authority, has a wrong concept of his authority, lazy, fearful of rebuke, blames others (mainly the wife), justifies himself, leans on wife, is a "Mama's Boy," relinquishes the spiritual authority over his house, and is irresponsible.

Behind each one of these traits there is a demon of the same name that needs to be cast out.

Casting Jezebel Out.

When a Jezebel manifests, it makes the woman sit up straight, raise her head and look down at you. You will notice she behaves with arrogance.

It is rare to be able to cast out one of these demons in the first ministry session. That is because the person receiving ministry needs to start walking in opposition to the demon.

It would be better if both husband and wife are ministered to at the same time, although not necessarily together. Some amount of counseling is needed to teach them how to oppose their demons of Ahab and Jezebel.

Counsel the woman that she needs to submit to the husband, stop controlling him, stop complaining about him to her friends. Stop arguing with him and instead agree with him in everything. She should start speaking highly of her husband. Let him make all the decisions, etc. She needs to oppose all the impulses and influence of Jezebel by doing exactly the opposite of that which the Jezebel nature dictates. Then her Jezebel will weaken and be easier to cast out.

If the husband is not receiving ministry, it will be more difficult for the woman to do all this on her own, but it is not impossible. The ideal situation is for them to both get rid of Jezebel and Ahab at the same time.

As the husband starts fighting his demon by being more responsible and mature, making the decisions, taking care of all the day to day problems that are more suited to a man's role to resolve, and opposes all Ahab thinking and all Ahab attitudes, his Ahab will also weaken and be easier to cast out.

My experience is that in casting out Jezebel, it is easier to first cast out all the demons that work with her, and then cast out Jezebel last. (But be listening to the Holy Spirit, He might direct otherwise.) As you cast out the demons under her, remind her that her "empire" is destroyed.

This spirit has lived through all ages of human-kind, and still resents the time when women covered their head as a sign of submission. Jezebel hates for the woman's head to be covered. If the manifesting Jezebel is strong, she will rip a scarf off the woman's head, and she won't allow the woman's head to be covered. Keeping it covered will help to weaken Jezebel.

I am assuming that the person reading this book has some experience in deliverance already. For those of you that have not seen deliverance being ministered, let me explain what happens when a scarf or kerchief, or even a piece of paper towel is put on the head of a woman that is being ministered deliverance. When the demon manifests, the demon looks out through the woman's eyes, uses the woman's mouth to speak, and the woman's hands or arms to push back the ministers or for other defensive or aggressive motions.

If the demon that manifests is a Jezebel, the demon will use the woman's hands to take the scarf off her head. At that moment, it is not the woman who does it, but the Jezebel demon in her.

First cast out the demons working with Jezebel (refer to the list of demons) as Pride, Arrogance, Haughtiness, Rebellion, Control, Domination, Scheming, Superiority, Center of Attention, Gossip, Jealousy, Argument, Strife, Witchcraft, Charismatic Witchcraft, Unsubmissiveness, Authoritarian, Do it My Way, Selfishness, Ego, Lust, Mother of Jezebel, Daughter of Jezebel, Daughter of Ahab, Mother of Ahab, etc.,

Then start casting out all the pagan goddesses by name, as highlighted in chapter 6 of this book, or refer to the list of demons.

Then command Jezebel to manifest and start casting her out. This demon will talk to you and might even threaten you. Remind her that your authority comes from the third heaven, at the right hand of the Father, in Christ Jesus. She might say "This woman is mine," or something similar. Remind her that the woman belongs to the Lord Jesus Christ. Remind Jezebel that her "empire" is destroyed, that she does not have any "servants" left.

Ask the Lord to send an eunuch to throw her out the window. Command the eunuch to throw Jezebel out in the name of Jesus. Then ask the Lord to send the angels with the dogs barking. Read her the Scriptures at the end of chapter 2, (*2 Kings 9: 30-35*). Ask the Lord for Jehu to come riding his horse and trample Jezebel. By now, Jezebel should be weak enough to be cast out, if she has not left already.

Command Jezebel to come out of all the parts of the female anatomy. This is the reason why I prefer women to minister to women, and men to men. I would not like a man ministering to me in this manner. Men have to be sensitive to women's feelings when they minister. The woman could be embarrassed.

Casting out Mother of Jezebel, Daughter of Jezebel, etc.

To cast out Mother of Jezebel, break the evil soul tie with the daughter and cast out the evil soul of the daughter. Do this first and Mother of Jezebel will not have a legal right to stay. Correspondingly, break first the evil soul tie with the mother to cast out Daughter of

Jezebel, then cast out the evil soul of the mother, and follow that by casting out Daughter of Jezebel. Repeat for Mother and Daughter of Ahab.

If you find out that the woman had a grandmother that was a witch, you need to break the evil soul tie with the grandmother and cast out the evil soul of the grandmother. Then cast out "grand-daughter of Jezebel." Sometimes the grandmother's influence is worse than the mother's influence or the father's influence.

I ministered to a lady whose father's real mother was a witch. This lady had very strong evil soul ties to both the father and to the grandmother, whom neither she nor her father ever met. The demon called granddaughter of Jezebel was there and was very strong. She received tremendous deliverance from that demon.

The Frightened Jezebel.

The typical manifestation of Jezebel is with a proud and arrogant attitude, as explained before. On one occasion, a friend of mine and I were ministering deliverance to a woman when a Jezebel manifested as very frightened. The more I commanded her to go, the more frightened she became. This was unusual so we stopped for a moment of prayer. The Holy Spirit told us that there was a principality holding the Jezebel back and would not let her go, and his name was Lucifer. This demon had come down from the heavenlies to defend the territory they had in the woman. It turned out that the woman had been a witch who had converted to Christianity, and had made a pact with Satan. Thus, the higher

demons did not want her delivered. She finally received
deliverance.

Do Not Be Deceived.

Jezebel is a demon that likes to pretend that she
has come out. When you command Jezebel out, and there
is a manifestation of a demon coming out, as coughing,
retching, etc, is quite probable that Jezebel kicked out
another demon under her command. The way to know if
she is still there, is to call her by name. She might not
answer the first or second time, but by the third or fourth
time that you call her, she will get angry and answer
something like: "What do you want?" Just continue casting her out, until you test and she does not answer any
longer.

When Jezebel is out, continue casting out minor
demons that work with Jezebel, until you are satisfied
that they all are gone. Then ask the Lord to fill the voids
with the spirits of God that are opposite of the spirits
that have left, such as humility (opposite of pride), holi-
ness (opposite of lust) etc.

Casting Out Ahab

First cast out Weakness, Weakness of Character,
Childishness, Little Boy, Pouting, Temper Tantrums,
Laziness, Fear of Rebuke, Self-Justification, Irresponsi-
bility, Lack of Authority, Fear of Authority, Mama's Boy,
Blaming Others, Blaming Wife, Leaning on Others, Lean-

ing on Wife, Fear of Working, Fear of Failure, etc., (Refer to the list of demons). Cast out Son of Ahab, Son of Jezebel, Father of Ahab, Father of Jezebel. For each one of these break the evil soul tie with the mother, father, daughter or son, and command the evil soul of the mother, father, daughter or son to come out. For instance, to cast out Son of Jezebel, break the evil soul tie with the man's mother, then cast out the evil soul of the mother. Then cast out Son of Jezebel.

For a son of Ahab, you have to break the evil soul tie with the man's father, and command the evil soul of the father to come out, then cast out Son of Ahab. If the man has sons and daughters, break the evil soul ties with them and command the evil soul of each of them out, **one by one,** and proceed as above, to cast out Father of Jezebel and Father of Ahab.

If the man had a grandmother that was a very strong Jezebel or a witch, break the evil soul tie with the grandmother and cast the evil soul of the grandmother out. Then cast out grandson of Jezebel. Break the evil soul tie with the grandfather (husband of the Jezebellic grandmother) also, and cast out grandson of Ahab.

Cast out Baal, Belial, Belus, Baalim, Merodach, Baal-Berith, Baal-Zebub, Osiris, Tammuz, and all the other names of gods. Refer to the names of the demons in chapter 7 of this book.

The list of names of Jezebel and Ahab demons in chapter 7 does not include all of the demons related to Ahab and Jezebel. Also, depending on the person you are ministering to, not all of the mentioned demons might be there. Or they might not be grouped in the way shown. Let the Holy Spirit guide you. The lists in this book are only intended as a guideline, they are not etched in stone.

There is blank space to the right of the list so that you can write any other names that come up as you minister. I have the impression that the demons may have taken other names upon themselves, of notorious, important historical women, such as empresses, queens or king's concubines.

I would like for you to write to me, or send me an e-mail with any additional names you find, so that I can update the list.

You can write to me at:

That Way of Jesus Ministries
P.O. Box 2854
Sugarland, Texas 77487-2854

Or, e-mail me at:

miramar0@flash.net

74

7

Names of Jezebel and Ahab Demons

Jezebel Demons

Daughter of Jezebel
Daughter of Ahab
Mother of Jezebel
Mother of Ahab

Sexual Impurity

Lust
Fantasy Lust
Defilement
Adultery
Fornication
Incest
Exposure
Frigidity
Smut
Filth
Oral Sex
Anal Sex
Sodomy
Take Me
Rape
Obscenity
Pornography
Child Pornography
Child Molestation
Pornographic Flashbacks
Pornographic Memory
Burning Passion
Harlotry
Prostitution
Sexual Incitement
Sexual Enticement
Lesbianism
Homosexuality
Bi-sexual

Cross Dresser
Transvestite
Exhibitionism
Flirting
Lust of the Eyes
Lust of the Flesh
Inordinate Affection
Nymphomania
Masturbation
Sadism
Masochism
Dominatrix
Satyrism
Seduction
Sensuality
Incubus
Perversity
Perverse Spirit
Cupid
Eros

Pride

Haughtiness
Ego
Self
Egotism
Conceit
Vanity
Self-Righteousness
Self-Importance, "The Queen"

Arrogance
Center of Attention
Superiority
Pride of Life
Self-Sufficiency
Pretension

Selfishness

Egoism
Egotism
Egocentric
Egomania
Number One
Self-Centered
Self-Obssesed
Self-Idolatry
Self-Admiration
Self-Approval
Self-Interest
Self-Concern
Self-Seeker
Taker, not Giver
People User
Inconsiderate
Narcissistic
Abortion
Child Abuse
Child Neglect
Child Abandonment
Child Murderer

Control

Possessiveness
Dominance
Deception
Ascendancy
Lying
Manipulation
Scheming
Strategy
String-pulling
Wire-pulling
Do it my way
Authoritarian
Tyrannical
Argumentative
Upper hand
Whip hand
Ruler
Master
Revenge

Witchcraft

Charismatic Witchcraft
White Magic
Black Magic
Sorcery
Fortune Telling
Horoscopes
Astrology
Tarot Cards

Crystal Ball
ESP
Mind Control
Conjurations
Incantations
Potions
Burning of dedicated candles
Channeling
Crystals
Wicca
Satanism
Charms
Fetishes
Levitation
Palmistry
Handwriting Analysis
Hair Reading
Iridiology
Automatic Handwriting
Ouija Board
Pendulum
Divination
Enchantment
Fire Gazing
Astral Projection
Kabala
Hypnosis
Medium
Psychic Powers
Psychokinesis

Telepathy
Table Tipping
Talismans
Fetishes
Santeria
Voodoo
"The Witch"
Poltergeist
Tea Leaf Reading
Palmistry
Curses
Hexes
Vexes

Criticism

Critical Spirit
Judgmental, judging
Accusation
Fault-Finding
Censure
Prejudice

Jealousy

Envy
Suspicion
Distrust
Covetousness
Greed
Discontent

Rebellion
>   Willfulness
>   Disobedience
>   Anti-submissiveness
>   Stubborness
>   Defiance
>   Opposition
>   Resistance
>   Obstinacy

Competition
>   I'm better than you
>   I am the Best
>   I win
>   What I think is the way it is
>   What I say is the way it is
>   I have the last word
>   I am more important
>   My choices are the best
>   I go in first
>   I know better
>   Competitive
>   Arguing
>   Driving
>   Pride
>   Ego
>   Headstrong
>   Intimidating
>   Strife
>   Contention
>   Disagreement

Debate
Altercation
Quarreling
Discussion
Controvert
Conflict
Dissension
Friction
Fighting
Battle
Clash
Combat
Dispute
Assert
Maintain
Insist

Retaliation

Destruction
Spite
Hatred
Malice
Treachery

Marriage-Breaking

Hatred of husband
Despising husband
Belittling
Lack of intimacy
Arguing

Contentious
Anti-submissiveness
Distance
Separation
Divorce
Asmodeus
Osmodeus
Matrimonial Discord
Never Satisfied

Child Abuse

Provocation
Disrespect of sons (or daughters)
Belittlement of sons (or daughters)
Humiliation of sons (or daughters)
Hatred of sons (or daughters)
Jealousy of sons (or daughters)
Negligence of sons (or daughters)
Destruction of sons (or daughters)
Physical abuse
Mental abuse
Emotional abuse
Psychological abuse
Verbal abuse
Sexual abuse
Incest
Abortion
Murder
Moloch

Names of Goddesses

(Note: although Delilah, Eve and Josephine are not goddesses, they have been added because they are found as demons among the demons of the goddesses. I believe Josephine refers to the wife of Napoleon)

Ashera
Asherim
Ashtaroth
Ashtoreth
Astoreth
Athirat
Astarte
Ashtoreth of the Sidonians
Ishtar
Goddess of the Groves
Athirat
Asterie
Astrea
Themis
Virgin Themis
The Perfect One
Goddess of Justice
Semiramis
Beltis
Queen of Heaven
Eve
Aphrodite

Mylitta
The Mediatrix
Woman Mediator
Melitza
Melissa
Rhea
Cybele
Melitta
Venus
Archia
Arkh
Diana
Diana of the Ephesians
Diana of the Romans
Artemis
Moon Goddess
Ash-Toret
Ash-Turit
Mother of the Gods
Minerva
Athena
Beltis
Goddess of Wisdom
Anahita
Ardvi Sura Anahita
Anat
Anath
Atargatis
Isis
Ceres

Shing-Moo
Sati
Virgin Mary
Re-Anen
Josephine
Delilah
St. Barbara
Aida-Odeo
Mother of the gods
Mother of lies
Mother of cheating
Inanna
Enheduanna
Gaia
Hather
Demeter
Kali
Ariadne

Goddesses of the Feminist Movement

Songi
Athena
Tara
Pasowee
Ishtar
Ixmucane
Aditi
Nashe

Wiccan Goddesses

Artemis
Astarte
Athene
Dione
Melusine
Aphrodite
Cerridwen
Dana
Arianhod
Isis
Bride
Changing Woman
Shakti
Semiramis
ImmaculatelyConceived Blessed Virgin Mary
Aida Odeo

(If you have cast out all the previous demons, cast out Jezebel now)

Ahab Demons

Son of Jezebel
Son of Ahab
Father of Jezebel
Father of Ahab

Passivity
    Laziness
    Inertia
    Lethargy
    Sloth
    Indolent
    Inactivity
    Avoiding work
    "I hate working"
    "Don't want to work"

Fear
    of responsibility
    of authority
    of rebuke
    of ridicule
    of failing
    Blaming wife
    Blaming others

Irresponsibility
> Unreliability
> Childishness
> Pouting
> Temper Tantrums
> Lassitude
> Undependability
> Carelessness
> Ineptitude
> Foolishness
> Little Boy
> Mama's Boy
> Good Old Boy
> Emasculation

Weakness
> Insecurity
> Indecision
> Compromise
> Lack of character
> Lack of authority
> Leaning on wife
> Leaning on others
> Milque-toast

Sexual Impurity
> Lust
> Fantasy lust
> Defilement
> Adultery

Fornication
Incest
Exposure
Impotence
Smut
Filth
Oral Sex
Anal Sex
Sodomy
Take Me
Rape
Obscenity
Pornography
Child Pornography
Child Molestation
Pornographic Flashbacks
Pornographic Memory
Burning Passion
Prostitution
Sexual Enticement
Sexual Incitement
Homosexuality
Lesbianism
Bi-sexual
Cross-dresser
Transvestite
Exhibitionist
Flirting
Lust of the Eyes
Lust of the Flesh

Inordinate Affection
Masturbation
Sadism
Masochism
Effeminate
Satyrism
Seduction
Sensuality
Succubus
Perversion
Perverse Spirit

Names of the gods

Baal
Baalim
Bel
Belial
Perseus
Phoroneus
Nimrod
Nin
Tammuz
Lord of Heaven
The Sun
Belus
Merodach
Osiris
Horus
Apis

Saturn
Baal-Berith
Baal-Zebub
Baal-Sutekh
El-Berith
Lord of the Flies
Kronos
"Bread of Life"
Nin
Ninus
Dyonisius
Bacchus
Iacchus
Siva, Shiva
Moloch

(If you have cast out the previous demons, cast Ahab out now.)

FRANK HAMMOND ...
ENDORSEMENT

The Jezebel spirit is an especially diabolical, deceptive, intimidating spirit of control, too often unrecognized, and unconfronted. Jezebel wreaks havoc in homes and work-places. Jezebelian witchcraft destroys ministries, unless dealt with swiftly and boldly by those in authority. When working through leadership, she leaves many wounded and confused.

I thank God for this book and its exposure of the wiles of the devil through the Jezebel spirit.

Frank Hammond,
The Children's Bread Ministry

Impac
Chris **ian**
Books

332 Leffingwell Ave., Suite 101
Kirkwood, MO 63122

AVAILABLE AT YOUR LOCAL BOOKSTORE, OR YOU MAY
ORDER DIRECTLY. Toll-Free, order-line only M/C, DISC,
or VISA 1-800-451-2708.

Visit our Website at *www. impactchristianbooks.com*

Write for *FREE* Catalog.